Tennessee Waltz

Q ★ U ★ I ★ L ★ T

by Sue Bouchard

To Ken, My dance partner in life.
                    Love, Sue

Pieced by Sue Bouchard
Quilted by Sandy Thompson
58" x 58"

Second printing February, 2004
Published by Quilt in a Day®, Inc
1955 Diamond Street, San Marcos, CA 92078
©2003 by Eleanor A. Burns Family Trust

ISBN 1-891776-15-0

Art Director Merritt Voigtlander
Production Artist Marie Harper
Editor Eleanor Burns

Table of Contents

History

Tennessee Waltz is another name for a traditional quilt pattern called "54-40 or Fight." The pattern was named after a campaign slogan used by James Polk, the victorious Democratic candidate in 1844. It stands for 54 degrees, 40 minutes north latitude. This was the Oregon Territory border that was subject to dispute with Great Britain. The proponents of this slogan wanted the United States to have this territory or else go to war.

Many old quilt pattern names were based on political opinions and controversies. Ruth Finley pointed out in her book, *Old Patchwork Quilts and the Women Who Made Them,* "The fact that women might not vote did not mean that they were ignorant of the government…Why else should they have expressed, as they did, their political approbation and party loyalty in the naming of their favorite patchwork?" Other patterns named after political feelings of the same time period are "Lincoln's Platform", after the President's stand on slavery, and the "Whig's Rose" named after the Whig party that was formed to oppose Andrew Jackson and the Democratic Party in 1834.

As Ruth Finley also points out in *Old Patchwork Quilts,* quilt pattern names have a tendency to change in different locations across the country. She calls it "The Migration of Patterns". As people moved, the design of the pattern stayed the same, but a different name was given based on new surroundings and interests. This may explain how the pattern "54-40 or Fight" gained the name "Tennessee Waltz."

Let the music begin!

Sue Bouchard

4

The illusion of curved piecing in the Tennessee Waltz quilt is the result of combining a Star block with a Snowball block. As your eyes travel from one block to another, the pattern appears to dance across the quilt.

Pieced and Quilted by Sandy Thompson
56" x 74"

Selecting Your Fabrics

You can achieve two different looks to the quilts in this book. Both quilts use the same technique but differ in the use of fabric values.

First Variation

Traditional Scrappy Quilt with Octogon Snowball Blocks

This quilt uses the original 54-40 or Fight Star block.

 Choose the same Background for Star Points and Snowball Corners in a medium small-scale print that appears almost solid from a distance. Your Snowball block appears to be an octagon.

 Choose Star Points in a value darker than the above fabric. It should also appear solid from a distance.

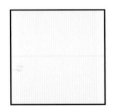 Choose the same Background fabric for both the Four-Patches and the Snowball blocks.

 Unique to this quilt is the scrappy Four-Patches. Select a variety of fabrics equal to the yardage for the Four-Patches.

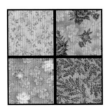 In addition, select a variety of fabrics for the Center block equal to the number of Star blocks in the quilt.

Pieced by Eleanor Burns
Quilted by Judy Jackson

58" x 75"

Second Variation

Contemporary Planned Quilt with Kaleidoscope Snowball Blocks.

This quilt uses fewer fabrics. The result is an open, airy design.

Choose a small to medium scale print with a variety of colors for the Four-Patches and Optional Pieced Border. This fabric should be medium in value.

Star Points are most effective if you choose a medium or dark fabric, which appears solid from a distance.

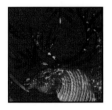

Choose a large-scale print with the same value and color family as the Star for the Star Centers and Outside Border.

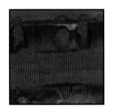

Fabric for Snowball Corners should be from a different color family which complements the Four-Patches. The fabric is repeated in the First Border.

Choose the same Background fabric for Four-Patches, Star Point Background and Snowball blocks.

A solid appearing Binding fabric makes a nice finish to the quilt.

Pieced by Sue Bouchard
Quilted by Sandy Thompson

59" x 76"

Block Yardage

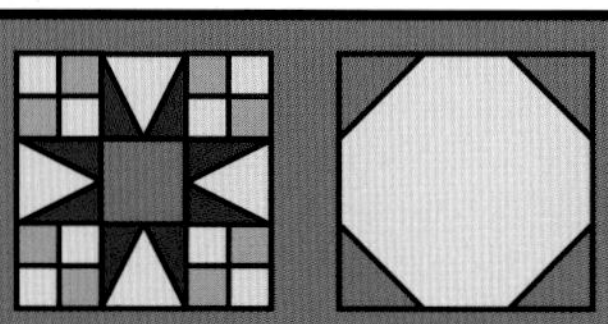	Two Star Runner 19" x 36" 2 Stars 1 Snowball	Three Star Runner 19" x 54" 3 Stars 2 Snowball	Wallhanging 3 x 3 – 41" x 41" 5 Stars 4 Snowball	Crib 3 x 5 – 41" x 59" 8 Stars 7 Snowball
Background	¾ yd	1⅛ yds	½ yd	1 yd
Four-Patch	(1) 2" strip cut in half	(2) 2" strips cut in half	(2) 2" strips cut in half	(4) 2" strips cut in half
Snowball Blocks	(1) strip x size of block cut later	(2) strips x size of block cut later	(1) strip x size of block cut later	(2) strips x size of block cut later
Corners and Rectangles	(1) 3½" strip	(2) 3½" strips		
Star Background	(1) 4" strip	(1) 4" strip	¼ yd (2) 4" strips	¼ yd (2) 4" strips
Star Points	¼ yd (1) 5" strip	¼ yd (1) 5" strip	⅓ yd (2) 5" strips	⅓ yd (2) 5" strips
Star Center	⅛ yd (2) 3½" squares	⅛ yd (3) 3½" squares	⅛ yd (1) 3½" strip cut into (5) 3½" squares	⅛ yd (1) 3½" strip cut into (8) 3½" squares
Four-Patch	⅛ yd (1) 2" strip cut in half	⅛ yd (2) 2" strips cut in half	¼ yd (2) 2" strips cut in half	⅓ yd (4) 2" strips cut in half
Snowball Corners	¼ yd (2) 3½" strips cut into (16) 3½" squares	⅓ yd (3) 3½" strips cut into (24) 3½" squares	¼ yd (2) 3½" strips cut into (16) 3½" squares	⅜ yd (3) 3½" strips cut into (28) 3½" squares

Border Yardage

First Border	¼ yd (3) 2" strips	⅓ yd (4) 2" strips	⅓ yd (4) 2" strips	⅓ yd (4) 2" strips
Pieced Second Border Background and Four-Patch Color			¼ yd of each (3) 2" strips of each	¼ yd of each (3) 2" strips of each
Third Border			⅝ yd (4) 4½" strips	¾ yd (5) 4½" strips
Fourth Border				
Binding	⅓ yd (3) 2¾" strips	⅜ yd (4) 2¾" strips	½ yd (5) 3" strips	⅔ yd (6) 3" strips
Backing	¾ yd	1⅔ yds	2⅔ yds	2⅔ yds
Batting	24" x 40"	24" x 58"	48" x 48"	48" x 66"

	Lap	Twin	Double/Queen	King
	5 x 7 – 59" x 77" 18 Stars 17 Snowball	5 x 9 – 69" x 105" 23 Stars 22 Snowball	7 x 9 – 87" x 105" 32 Stars 31 Snowball	9 x 11 – 105" x 123" 50 Stars 49 Snowball
Background	2 yds	2½ yds	3 yds	4¾ yds

Four-Patch	(8) 2" strips
	   cut in half
		(10) 2" strips
		   cut in half
			(13) 2" strips
			   cut in half
				(20) 2" strips
				   cut in half

Snowball Blocks	(5) strips x size of block
	   cut later
		(6) strips x size of block
		   cut later
			(8) strips x size of block
			   cut later
				(13) strips x size of block
				   cut later

Corners and Rectangles				
Star Background	⅔ yd (5) 4" strips	¾ yd (6) 4" strips	1 yd (8) 4" strips	1¾ yds (13) 4" strips
Star Points	⅞ yd (5) 5" strips	1 yd (6) 5" strips	1¼ yds (8) 5" strips	2 yds (13) 5" strips

Star Center	¼ yd
	(2) 3½" strips cut into
	  (18) 3½" squares
		⅜ yd
		(3) 3½" strips cut into
		  (23) 3½" squares
			⅜ yd
			(3) 3½" strips cut into
			  (32) 3½" squares
				⅔ yd
				(5) 3½" strips cut into
				  (50) 3½" squares

Four-Patch	½ yd (8) 2" strips cut in half	¾ yd (10) 2" strips cut in half	1 yd (13) 2" strips cut in half	1¼ yds (20) 2" strips cut in half

Snowball Corners	¾ yd
	(6) 3½" strips cut into
	  (68) 3½" squares
		⅞ yd
		(8) 3½" strips cut into
		  (88) 3½" squares
			1⅓ yds
			(12) 3½" strips cut into
			  (124) 3½" squares
				2 yds
				(18) 3½" strips cut into
				  (196) 3½" squares

	Lap	Twin	Double/Queen	King
First Border	½ yd (7) 2" strips	⅔ yd (8) 2" strips	⅔ yd (9) 2" strips	¾ yd (11) 2" strips

Pieced Second Border
  Background and
  Four-Patch Color
	⅓ yd of each
	(4) 2" strips of each
		⅜ yd of each
		(5) 2" strips of each
			⅜ yd of each
			(6) 2" strips of each
				½ yd of each
				(7) 2" strips of each

Third Border	1 yd (7) 4½" strips	1 yd (8) 3½" strips	1¼ yds (9) 3½" strips	1¼ yds (11) 3½" strips
Fourth Border		1¾ yds (8) 6½" strips	2 yds (10) 6½" strips	2¼ yds (12) 6½" strips
Binding	¾ yd (7) 3" strips	⅞ yd (9) 3" strips	1 yd (10) 3" strips	1⅛ yds (12) 3" strips
Backing	4⅔ yds	6½ yds	7⅔ yds	11 yds
Batting	66" x 83"	77" x 113"	92" x 113"	113" x 131"

Cutting Strips

1. Press fabric.

2. Fold fabric in half, matching edges. Don't worry about the selvages lining up correctly as this is not always possible.

3. Lay fabric on cutting mat with most of it to the right. Make sure edge is lined up at the left. Lay the ¼" line on 6" x 24" ruler along edge, and straighten.

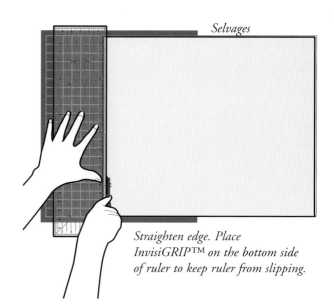

Straighten edge. Place InvisiGRIP™ on the bottom side of ruler to keep ruler from slipping.

4. Reposition ruler, and line up designated strip width. Cut Background, Four-Patch and Star fabrics using the 6" x 24" ruler. Cut Snowball strips using the cutting mat lines.

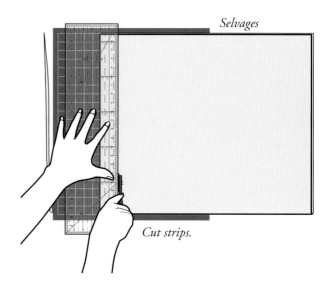

Cut strips.

5. Turn strip and square off selvage edges. Layer cut Star Centers and Snowball Corners into 3½" squares with 6" x 6" ruler.

6. Repeat until you have the desired number of squares.

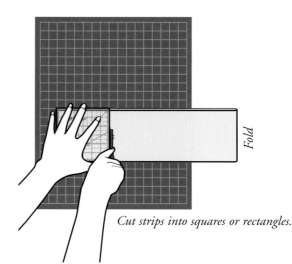

Cut strips into squares or rectangles.

Supplies

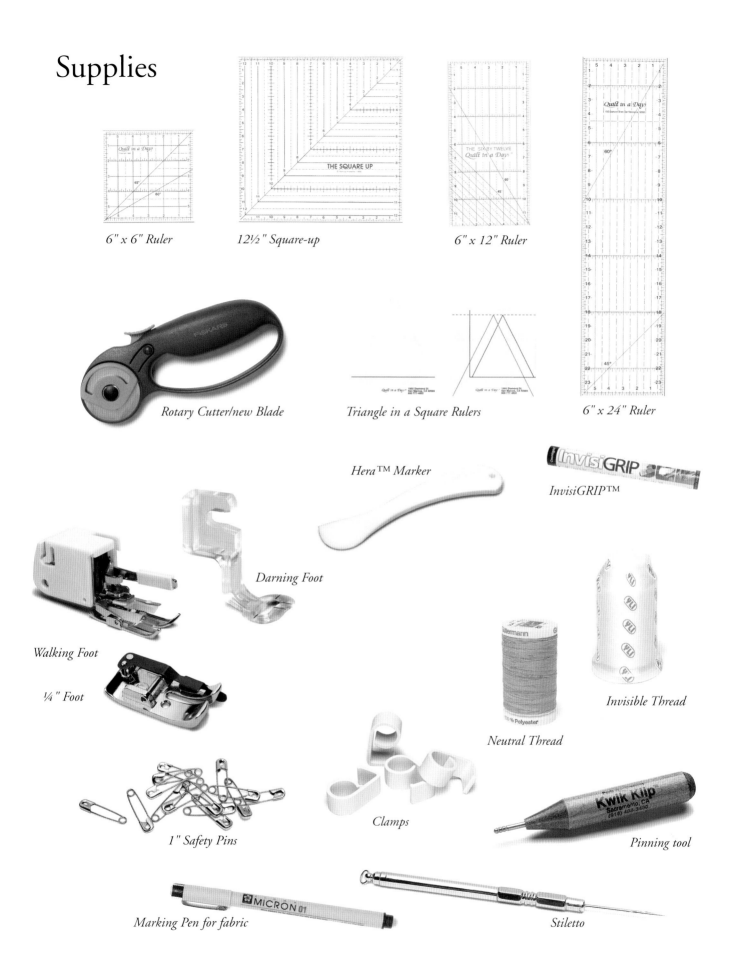

6" x 6" Ruler

12½" Square-up

6" x 12" Ruler

6" x 24" Ruler

Rotary Cutter/new Blade

Triangle in a Square Rulers

Hera™ Marker

InvisiGRIP™

Darning Foot

Walking Foot

¼" Foot

Invisible Thread

Neutral Thread

1" Safety Pins

Clamps

Pinning tool

Marking Pen for fabric

Stiletto

Paste-Up Sheet

Cut out small swatches of your fabrics and paste them in place with a glue stick to visualize how your finished blocks will look before you begin sewing.

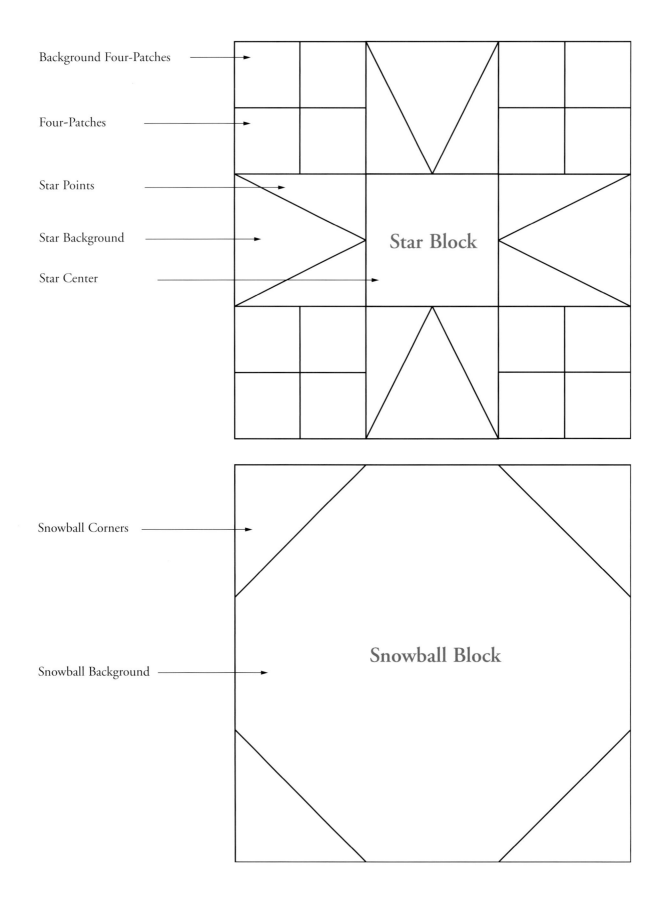

Background Four-Patches

Four-Patches

Star Points

Star Background

Star Center

Star Block

Snowball Corners

Snowball Background

Snowball Block

Making Four-Patches

Sew test set of strips. Width should measure 3½".

1. Place 2" Background Four-Patch strips right sides together to 2" Four-Patch strips.

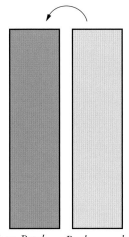

Four-Patch   Background

Number of Half Strips	
Two Star Tablerunner	2
Three Star Tablerunner	3
Wallhanging	4
Crib	7
Lap	16
Twin	20
Double/Queen	26
King	40

2. Using a ¼" seam allowance, sew half strips together.

3. Set seams with Four-Patch strip on top, open and press toward Four-Patch.

4. Measure width of strips. They should measure 3½".

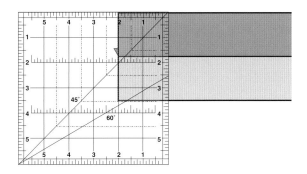

5. Layer first strip right side up on gridded cutting mat with Background across top. Place second strip right sides together to it with Four-Patch across top. Lock seams. Line up strips with grid.

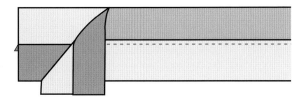

Follow illustrations exactly to end up with locking seams.

6. Square left end. Cut 2" pairs from each strip set.

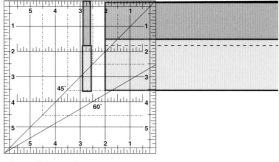

Cut 2" layered sections.

7. Stack on spare ruler to carry to sewing area.

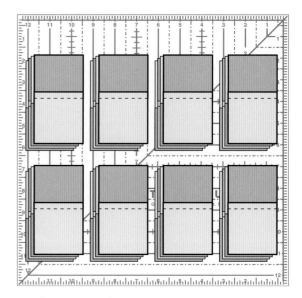

Stack 2" pairs and carry to sewing area.

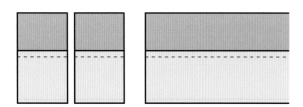

Number of Pairs	
Two Star Tablerunner	8
Three Star Tablerunner	12
Wallhanging	20
Crib	32
Lap	72
Twin	92
Double/Queen	128
King	200

8. Matching outside edges and center seam, assembly-line sew. Use stiletto to hold outside edges together and seams flat.

9. Repeat with all pieces for Four-Patches.

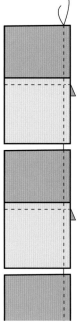

10. Remove the three stitches on each side of center indicated in red thread.

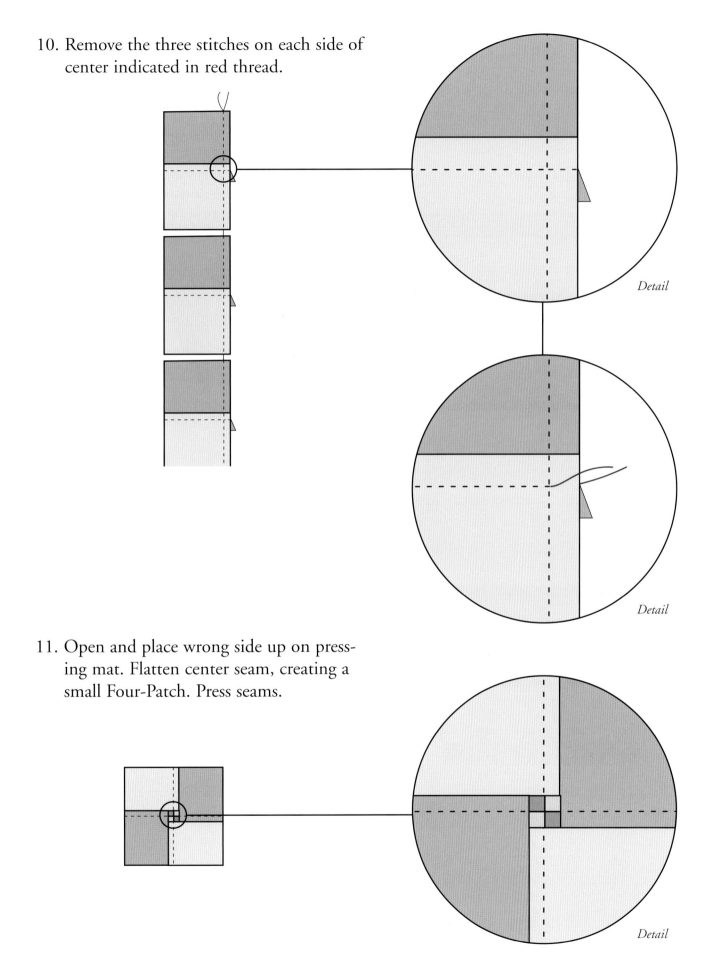

Detail

Detail

11. Open and place wrong side up on pressing mat. Flatten center seam, creating a small Four-Patch. Press seams.

Detail

Making Star Points

This pattern uses Triangle in a Square Rulers from Quilt in a Day. If you do not own these rulers, make your own templates from patterns on pages 28-29.

1. Keep 5" Star strips folded wrong sides together. This step is essential for mirror image pieces. Place selvage edges on left, and trim.

    fold

3. Layer cut on one diagonal. Sort these Star Points right side up.

2. With the 6" Square Up ruler, layer cut pairs of 2½" x 5" rectangles.

4. Layer 4" Background strips right side up. Place Triangle ruler or template on strip, accurately lining up the narrow part of the triangle with top of strip. The bottom is not as critical.

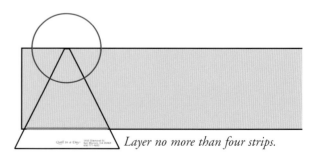

Layer no more than four strips.

Number of 2½" x 5" Pairs	
Two Star Tablerunner	4
Three Star Tablerunner	6
Wallhanging	10
Crib	16
Lap	36
Twin	46
Double/Queen	64
King	100

5. Cut Background triangles with rotary cutter, turning ruler with each cut.

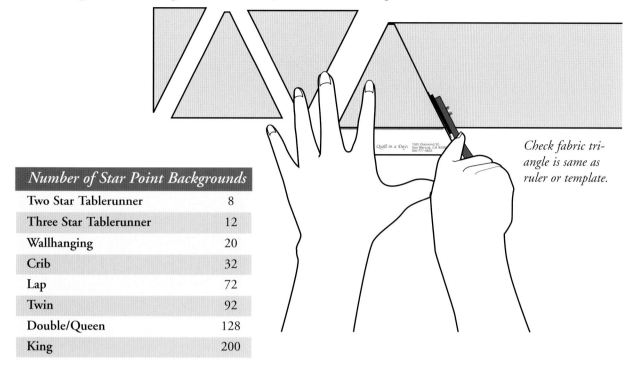

Check fabric triangle is same as ruler or template.

Number of Star Point Backgrounds	
Two Star Tablerunner	8
Three Star Tablerunner	12
Wallhanging	20
Crib	32
Lap	72
Twin	92
Double/Queen	128
King	200

6. Lay out Background Triangle with base at bottom. Position Star Points on both side of Background Triangle. Make sure all fabrics are turned right side up.

7. Set right Star Point stack aside. Flip Background Triangle right sides together to Star Point in left stack.

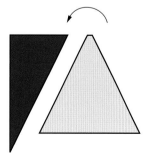

8. Position triangles so Star extends beyond Background at top, creating a tip at flat top. Star also extends at bottom.

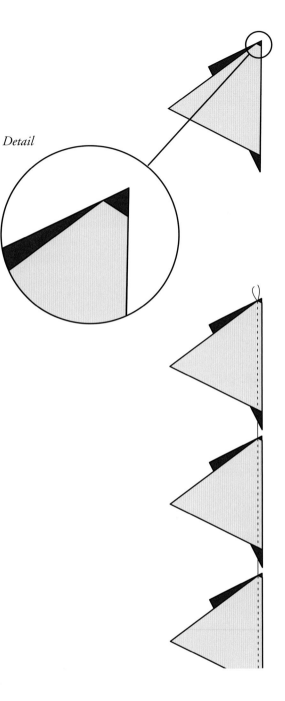

Detail

9. Assembly-line sew with ¼" seam allowance. Use stiletto to guide pieces.

10. Place on pressing mat with Star on top. Set seams, open and press toward Star.

11. Place remaining Star Point stack to right of Background Triangle.

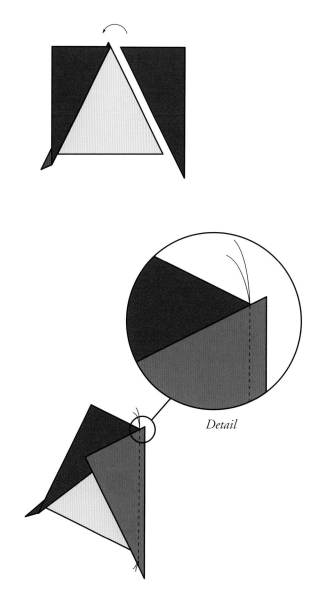

Detail

12. Flip right sides together, lining top tip of both pieces together. Assembly-line sew.

13. Set seams with Star on top, open, and press toward Star.

Squaring Up Patches

Patches are squared to 3½" with seam ¼" from top, and ⅛" from corners.

1. Place square ruler or template on patch. Line up red triangle lines on ruler with seams.

3. Turn patch. Do not turn ruler. Line up red 90° lines with left and bottom edges of patch. Trim patch on remaining two sides to 3½" square.

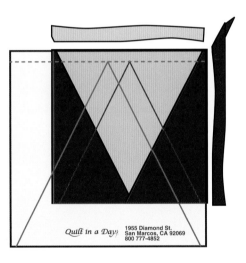

2. Trim patch on right side and top.

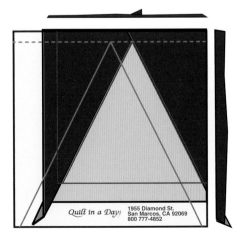

4. Seams on trimmed patch are ¼" from top, and ⅛" from corners.

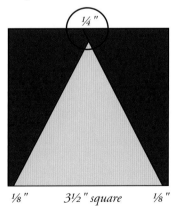

Sewing Star Blocks Together

1. Count out Star Points and 3½" Star Center squares with 3½" Four-Patches. Stack pieces per Star.

Number of Patches per Stack	
Two Star Tablerunner	2
Three Star Tablerunner	3
Wallhanging	5
Crib	8
Lap	18
Twin	23
Double/Queen	32
King	50

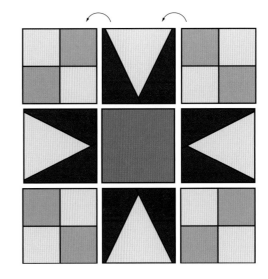

2. Flip middle vertical row to patches on left.

3. Matching outside edges, assembly-line sew.

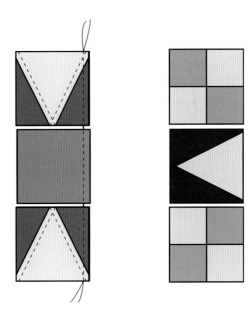

4. Flip right vertical row to middle row.

5. Assembly-line sew.

6. Clip apart after each Star, or every third row.

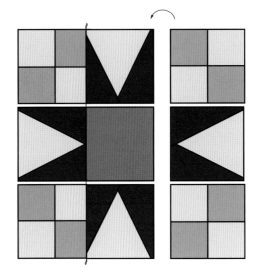

7. Turn block one quarter turn. Flip row on right to middle row. Press seams away from Star Points, and lock together. Pin.

8. Assembly-line sew.

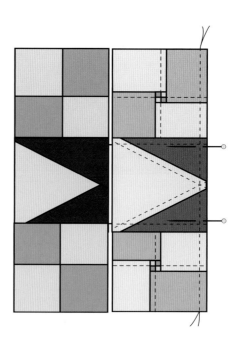

9. Sew last row, pressing and pinning seams away from Star Points.

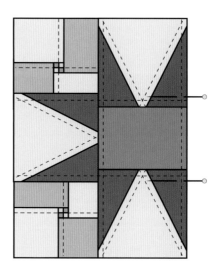

10. Clip Stars apart.

11. Press final seams away from center row.

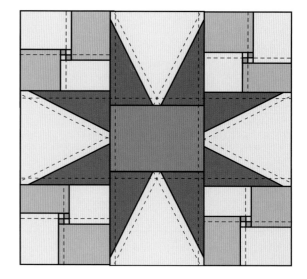

Making Snowball Block

1. Measure several Star blocks.

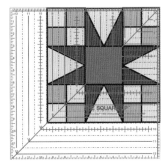

Record your average Measurement:_____

Approximately 9½"

2. Cut strips the size of your Star block from your Background fabric.

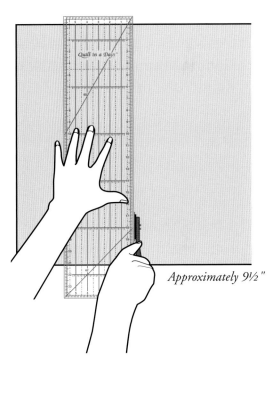

Number of Strips	
Two Star Tablerunner	1
Three Star Tablerunner	2
Wallhanging	1
Crib	2
Lap	5
Twin	6
Double/Queen	8
King	13

Approximately 9½"

3. Cut squares the size of your Star block from your strips.

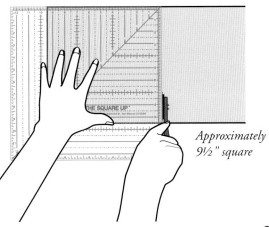

Number of Snowball Blocks	
Two Star Tablerunner	4
Three Star Tablerunner	6
Wallhanging	4
Crib	7
Lap	17
Twin	22
Double/Queen	31
King	49

Approximately 9½" square

23

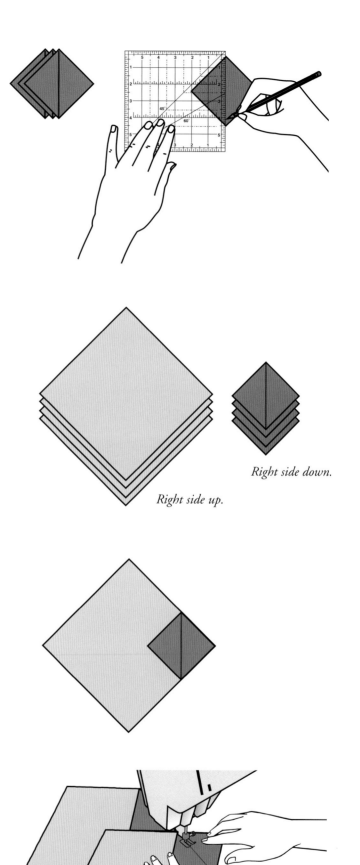

4. On the wrong side of the 3½" Snowball Corners, draw a diagonal line. Optional: Press in half wrong sides together on diagonal.

Number of Snowball Corners	
Two Star Tablerunner	16
Three Star Tablerunner	24
Wallhanging	16
Crib	28
Lap	68
Twin	88
Double/Queen	124
King	196

5. Place a stack of Background Squares right side up on point. Stack the Snowball Corners right side down.

Right side down.

Right side up.

6. Place a Snowball Corner right sides together to Background Square's corner. Match the corners.

7. Sew on the drawn line.

8. Assembly-line sew as many as manageable.

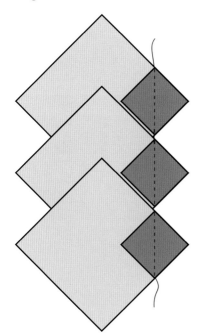

9. Turn and sew Snowball Corners on opposite corners.

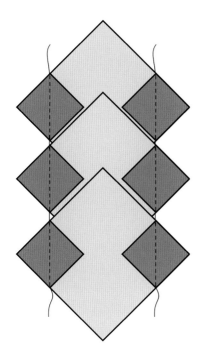

10. Clip apart.

11. Continue to sew Snowball Corners to remaining two corners. Clip apart.

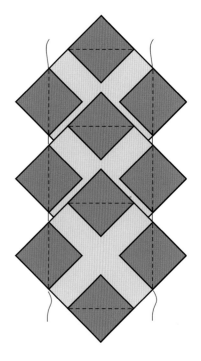

12. Place ¼" line on 6" x 12" ruler on stitching line. Trim off excess fabric to ¼" seam on all four corners.

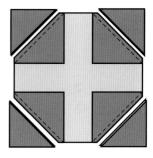

13. Press seams toward Snowball Corners.

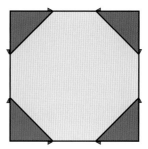

To complete Tablerunner, turn to page 42.

Sewing Top Together

1. Alternating Star and Snowball blocks, lay out the quilt top. Place a Star block in each corner.

   Layout examples for all size quilts are on pages 28 and 29.

2. Flip Row Two to Row One.

Lap example

3. Match and pin Star Points with Snowball Corners. Assembly-line sew.

4. Repeat process until all rows are completed.

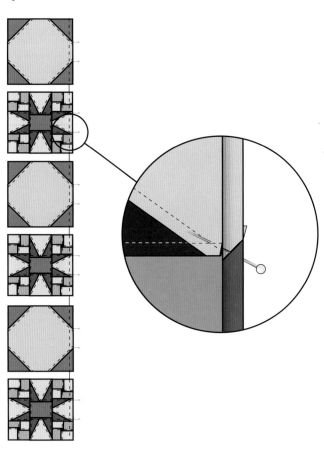

5. Press seams toward Snowball blocks.

6. Flip two horizontal rows together.

7. Lock and pin seams.

8. Sew remaining rows, consistently locking seams and matching Star Points.

9. Press quilt first on wrong side, then on right side.

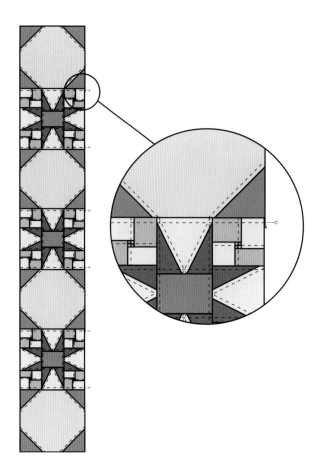

Triangle in a Square Templates

The Triangle in a Square Rulers are available on heavy acrylic from Quilt in a Day. Cutting with these rulers makes the process easier, and cut pieces are more accurate.

If you do not have these rulers, tape template plastic to these pages, trace templates with sharp markers, and cut out on the outside lines.

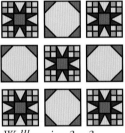

Wallhanging 3 x 3

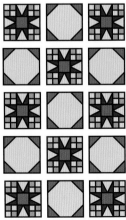

Crib 3 x 5

Lap 5 x 7

Twin 5 x 9

When indicated to use Triangle in a Square Rulers, trace around the triangle template with a marking pen, and rotary cut on the lines with a 6" x 12" Ruler.

Tape the square template to the underneath upper right corner of an acrylic 3½" or 6" x 6" Ruler and use as instructed.

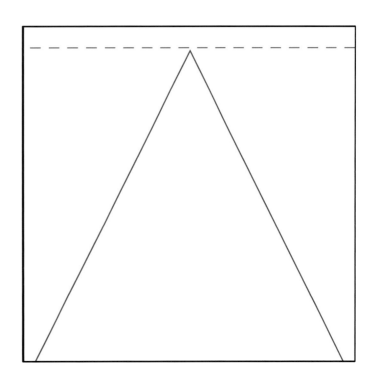

Double/Queen 7 x 9

King 9 x 11

Adding Borders

1. Trim selvage ends from First Border strips.

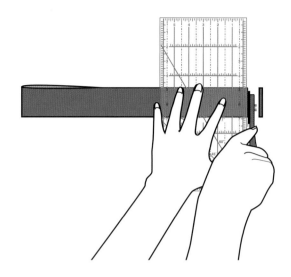

2. Piece strips together to desired length.

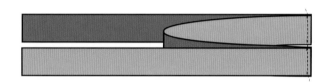

3. Pin and sew First Border to sides of quilt. Press seams to Border. Trim ends even.

4. Pin and sew First Border to top and bottom. Press seams toward Border. Trim ends even.

Making the Optional Pieced Second Border

1. Cut the Second Border 2" strips in half on fold line.

Number of Half Strips	
Wallhanging	5
Crib	6
Lap	8
Twin	9
Double/Queen	11
King	13

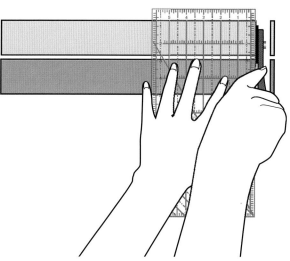

2. Place 2" light strips with 2" medium strips right sides together. Using a ¼" seam allowance, sew half strips together.

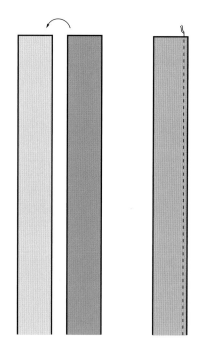

3. Set seams with medium on top, open and press toward medium.

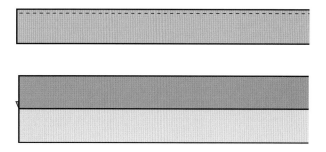

4. Layer strip sets on gridded cutting mat, offsetting seams ½".

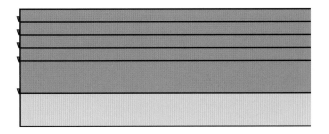

5. Cut into 2" pairs.

Number of Pairs	
Wallhanging	42
Crib	54
Lap	78
Twin	90
Double/Queen	102
King	126

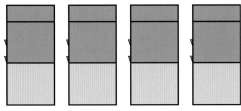

Cut 2" layered sections.

6. Sew pairs together end to end to make sides and top and bottom Borders.

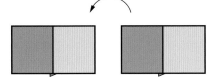

Number of Pairs for Borders		
	Sides	Top and Bottom
Wallhanging	10	11
Crib	16	11
Lap	22	17
Twin	28	17
Double/Queen	28	23
King	34	29

7. Press seams in the same direction.

Adding Optional Second Pieced Border

1. Pin Pieced Borders to sides of quilt. Make sure seams are going in same direction as arrows.

2. Sew with Pieced Border wrong side up.

3. Press toward First Border.

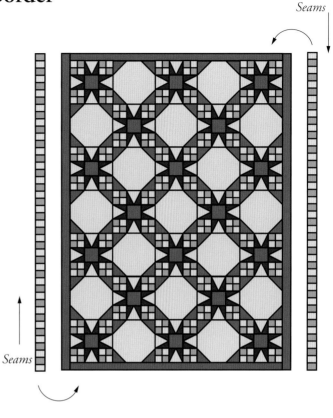

Seams

Seams

Seams

4. Repeat process with top and bottom Pieced Border.

5. Press toward First Border.

Seams

Seams

33

Adding Third Border

1. Trim selvage edges.

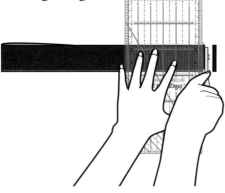

2. Piece Borders together to desired length for sides and top and bottom.

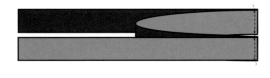

3. Sew side Borders to quilt first, then top and bottom Borders.

4. Press seams toward Border.

Adding Fourth Border

Twin, Double/Queen and King Only

1. Trim selvage edges.

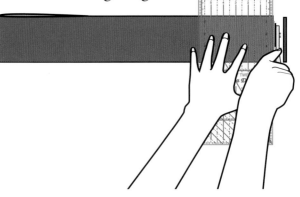

2. Piece Borders together to desired length for sides and top and bottom.

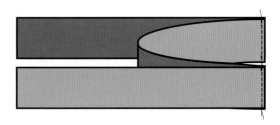

3. Sew side Borders to quilt first, then top and bottom Borders.

4. Press seams toward Border.

Machine Quilting

Layering the Quilt

1. Spread out Backing on a large table or floor area, right side down. Clamp fabric to edge of table with quilt clips, or tape Backing to the floor. Do not stretch Backing.

2. Layer the Batting on the Backing and pat flat.

3. With quilt right side up, center on the Backing. Smooth until all layers are flat. Clamp or tape outside edges.

Marking Stencil

1. Select a stencil which fits in open areas. Center stencil on area, and trace lines with water erasable fabric marking pen.

   Stencils designed for Double Wedding Ring quilts in 8" size fit perfectly inside Snowball blocks.

This stencil is HOL-001-08 from The Stencil Company™.

Safety Pinning

1. Place pin covers on 1" safety pins. Safety pin through all layers three to five inches apart. Pin away from marked quilting lines.

2. Catch tip of pin in grooves on pinning tool, and close pins.

3. Use pinning tool to open pins when removing them. Store pins opened.

"Stitch in the Ditch" with Walking Foot

1. Thread your machine with matching thread or invisible thread. If you use invisible thread, loosen top tension. Match the bobbin thread to the Backing.

2. Attach your walking foot, and lengthen the stitch to 8 to 10 stitches per inch or 3.0 to 3.5 on computerized machines.

3. Stitch in the ditch following quilting path.

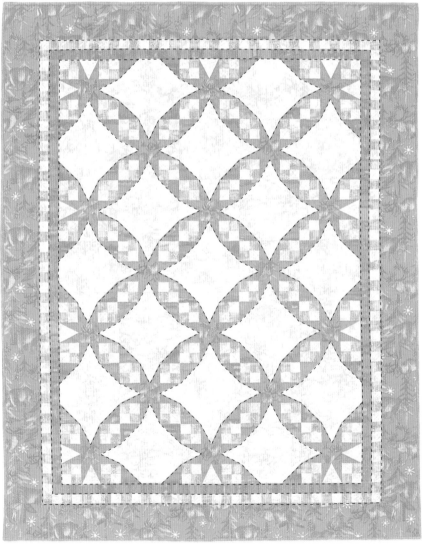

Example of machine quilting path

Quilting Snowball Block with Darning Foot

1. Attach darning foot to sewing machine. Drop feed dogs or cover feed dogs with a plate. No stitch length is required as you control the length. Use a fine needle and invisible or regular thread in the top and regular thread to match the Backing in the bobbin. Loosen top tension if using invisible thread.

2. Place hands flat on sides of marking. Bring bobbin thread up on line. Lock stitch and clip thread tails.

3. Free motion stitch around design.

4. Lock stitch and cut threads.

Quilting Star Block with Darning Foot

1. Place hands flat on sides of Star. Bring bobbin thread up at starting point.

2. Continuously stitch in the ditch following quilting pattern, without turning Star.

3. Lock stitch and cut threads.

● *Starting/Ending point*

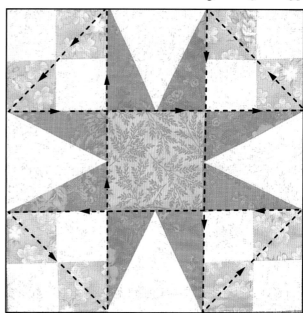

Binding

1. Place walking foot attachment on sewing machine and regular thread on top and in bobbin to match Binding.

2. Square off selvage edges, and sew 3" Binding strips together lengthwise. Fold and press in half with wrong sides together.

3. Line up raw edges of folded Binding with raw edges of quilt in middle of one side. Begin stitching 4" from end of Binding. Sew with 10 stitches per inch, or 3.0 to 3.5 on computerized machine. Sew ⅜" from edge, or width of walking foot.

4. At corner, stop stitching ⅜" in from edge with needle in fabric. Raise presser foot and turn quilt toward corner. Put foot back down. Stitch diagonally off edge of Binding.

5. Raise foot, and pull quilt forward slightly. Turn quilt to next side.

6. Fold Binding strip straight up on diagonal. Fingerpress diagonal fold.

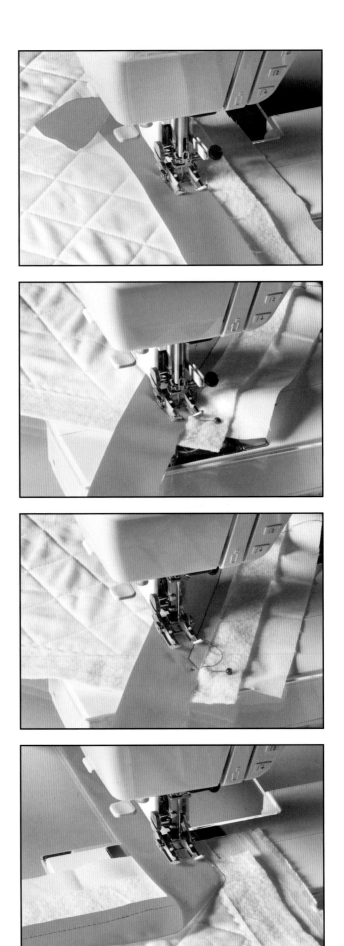

7. Fold Binding strip straight down with diagonal fold underneath. Line up top of fold with raw edge of Binding underneath.

8. Begin sewing from edge.

9. Continue stitching and mitering corners around outside of quilt.

10. Stop stitching 4" from where ends will overlap.

11. Line up two ends of Binding. Trim excess with ½" overlap.

12. Open out folded ends and pin right sides together. Sew a ¼" seam.

13. Continue stitching Binding in place.

14. Trim Batting and Backing up to ⅛" from raw edges of Binding.

15. Fold back Binding.

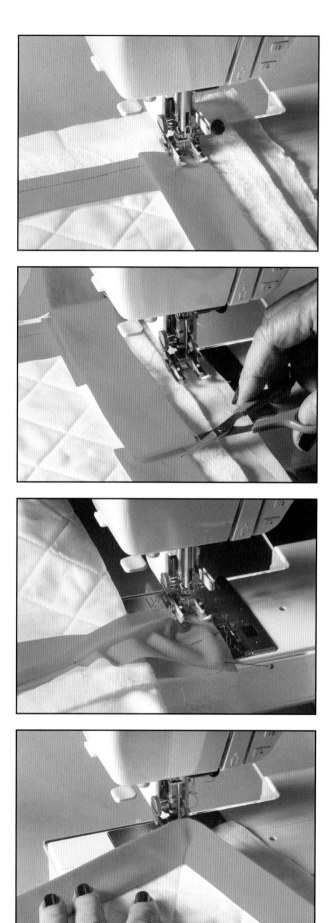

16. Fold Binding to back side of quilt. Pin in place so that folded edge on Binding covers stitching line. Tuck in excess fabric at each miter on diagonal.

17. From right side, "stitch in the ditch" using invisible thread on front side, and bobbin thread to match Binding on back side.

18. Catch folded edge of Binding on the back side with stitching. Optional: Hand stitch Binding in place.

19. Hand stitch miter.

20. Sew identification label on Back.

Tablerunners

Sue Bouchard pieced and quilted this Tablerunner in shades of blue and maroon, perfect for decorating any dining room table. The kaleidoscope Snowballs provide an excellent place to showcase free motion quilting.

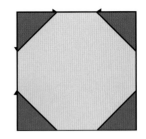

Completing the Table Runner

1. Set aside Snowball blocks to complete runner.

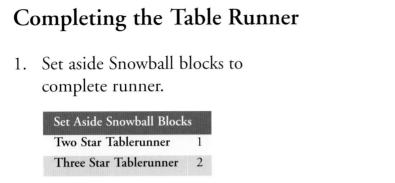

Set Aside Snowball Blocks	
Two Star Tablerunner	1
Three Star Tablerunner	2

2. Cut 3½" strip from side of remaining Snowball blocks.

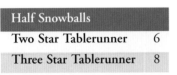

Snowball Blocks to Cut	
Two Star Tablerunner	3
Three Star Tablerunner	4

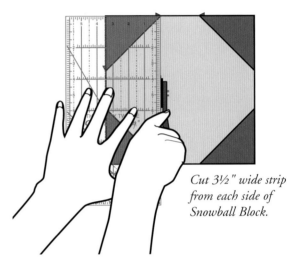

Cut 3½" wide strip from each side of Snowball Block.

3. Turn and cut 3½" strip from other side of Snowball block.

Half Snowballs	
Two Star Tablerunner	6
Three Star Tablerunner	8

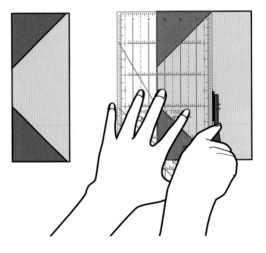

4. A small center piece is left over. This piece is not needed for the Tablerunner.

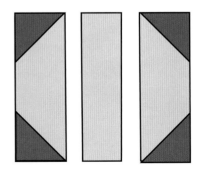

5. Cut 3½" Background strips into 3½" Corner squares and 3½" x 9½" Side Rectangles.

Two Star Tablerunner

Number of	Rectangles	Corners
Two Star Tablerunner	2	4
Three Star Tablerunner	4	4

6. Lay out patches needed to complete Tablerunner.

You Need	Star Blocks	Snowballs	Half Snowballs	Rectangles	Corners
Two Star Tablerunner	2	1	6	2	4
Three Star Tablerunner	3	2	8	4	4

Two Star Tablerunner

Three Star Tablerunner

7. Flip Row Two to Row One. Pin to match Star Points with Snowball Corners. Assembly-line sew.

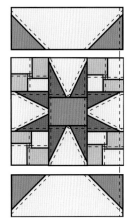

43

8. Repeat process until all rows are completed.

9. Press seams toward Snowball blocks so seams lock.

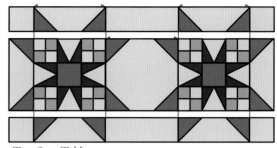

Two Star Tablerunner

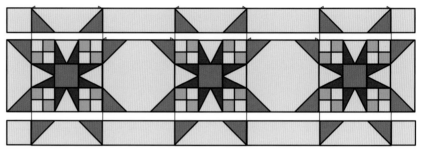

Three Star Tablerunner

10. Flip remaining rows together. Lock and pin seams, and sew.

11. Press seams away from middle row.

Two Star Tablerunner

Two Star Tablerunner

12. Sew Border to top and bottom, and then sides.

13. Set seams and press toward Border.

Two Star Tablerunner

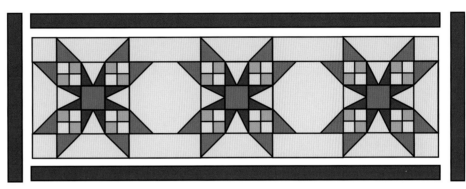

Three Star Tablerunner

Marking Straight Lines

1. Place ruler on desired straight quilting line.

2. Firmly push Hera™ Marker along edge of ruler, and mark crease.

3. Turn to **Machine Quilting** on page 35.

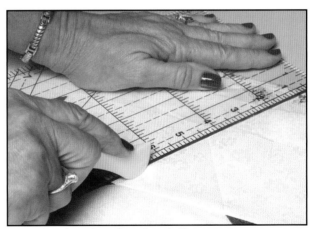

Extend quilting lines from Snowball pattern into Border rectangles.

Index

Pieced and Quilted
by Teresa Varnes
41" x 41"

Acknowledgments

Thank you for all your help and support throughout the development of this book.

Eleanor Burns
Lori Forsythe
Judy Jackson
Cynthia Martin
Dylan Mayer

Laurie McCauley
Sandy Thompson
Teresa Varnes
And all of my test students

A special thanks to the Rancho Buena Vista Adobe for their permission to use their location for the photos in the book.

Order Information

Quilt in a Day books offer a wide range of techniques and are directed toward a variety of skill levels. If you do not have a quilt shop in your area, you may write or call for a complete catalog and current price list of all books and patterns published by Quilt in a Day®, Inc.

Easy

Bits & Pieces Quilt
Courthouse Steps Quilt
Double Pinwheel
Easy Strip Tulip
Flying Geese Quilt in a Day
Irish Chain in a Day
Make a Quilt in a Day Log Cabin
Nana's Garden Quilt
Northern Star
Rail Fence Quilt
Star for all Seasons Placemats
Trip Around the World Quilt
Winning Hand Quilt

Applique

Applique in a Day
Dresden Plate Quilt
Sunbonnet Sue Visits Quilt in a Day
Spools & Tools Wallhanging
Dutch Windmills Quilt
Grandmother's Garden Quilt
Ice Cream Cone Quilt

Intermediate

Bears in the Woods
Birds in the Air Quilt
Boston Common
Delectable Mountains Quilt
Fans & Flutterbys
Friendship Quilt
Intermediate
Jewel Box
Kaleidoscope Quilt
Lover's Knot Quilt

Machine Quilting Primer
May Basket Quilt
Morning Star Quilt
Snowball Quilt
Star Log Cabin Quilt
Trio of Treasured Quilts
Triple Irish Chain Quilts
Wild Goose Chase Quilt

Holiday

Christmas Quilts and Crafts
Country Christmas
Country Flag
Last Minute Gifts
Log Cabin Wreath Wallhanging
Log Cabin Christmas Tree Wallhanging
Lover's Knot Placemats
Patchwork Santa
Stockings & Small Quilts

Sampler

Block Party Series 3, Quilters Almanac
Block Party Series 4, Christmas Traditions
Block Party Series 5, Pioneer Sampler
Block Party Series 6, Applique in a Day
Block Party Series 7, Stars Across America
Star Spangled Favorites
Still Stripping After 25 Years
Town Square Sampler
Underground Railroad

Angle Piecing

Blazing Star Tablecloth
Pineapple Quilt
Radiant Star Quilt

Quilt in a Day®, Inc. • 1955 Diamond Street • San Marcos, CA 92078
1 800 777-4852 • Fax: (760) 591-4424 • www.quiltinaday.com

Color Variations

For a different look, try using a dark fabric for your Background. Your Four-Patches, Star Points and Snowball blocks simply glow on the black.

Pieced and quilted by Sue Bouchard
38" x 55"

For a great Crib quilt, select a border fabric with many bright colors. For each set of Star Points, choose one of the bright colors from the border fabric. Keep the Star Centers the same for all the Star Blocks.

Pieced by Sue Bouchard
Quilted by Cynthia Martin
32" x 50"